Book n° 26

26 Alphabets and 26 Activities

BOOK FOR KIDS
Ages 3 - 6

56 pages and 8,5 x 11 in

This book belongs to:

....

....

....

Introduction:

Indeed, the number **26** refers to the number of alphabets. With each alphabet, we prepared an activity. And while doing these activities, kids become familiar with the **26** alphabets easily. In fact, kids are to trace alphabets, and sometimes they are to color these alphabets and drawings; and on other pages, kids are to find the right alphabet.

This book is divided into two parts. Concerning the first part, kids are to deal with **26** alphabets activities. Then in the second part, we present for kids **26** different other alphabets activities so as to give them more chances to learn and get fun.

This book is composed of 56 pages and it is perfectly sized at 8,5x11 in.

Really, this book is very useful for kids between ages 3 and 6. So, if kids want to learn easily the English alphabets and with pleasure without being bored at all, then this is the right book. Kids will certainly get fun, enjoyment and benefit from this interesting book .

As we know, kids love such activities; that's why we prepared this kind of books so as to give them this chance and let them live great moments of happiness and fun.

Please, if you have any remark about this book, do not hesitate to send us an email via: apamog@hotmail.com

THANK YOU

Part n° 01:

26 ALPHABETS

AND

26 ACTIVITIES

Aa

alligator

Color the letters Bb

Trace and write the letters Bb

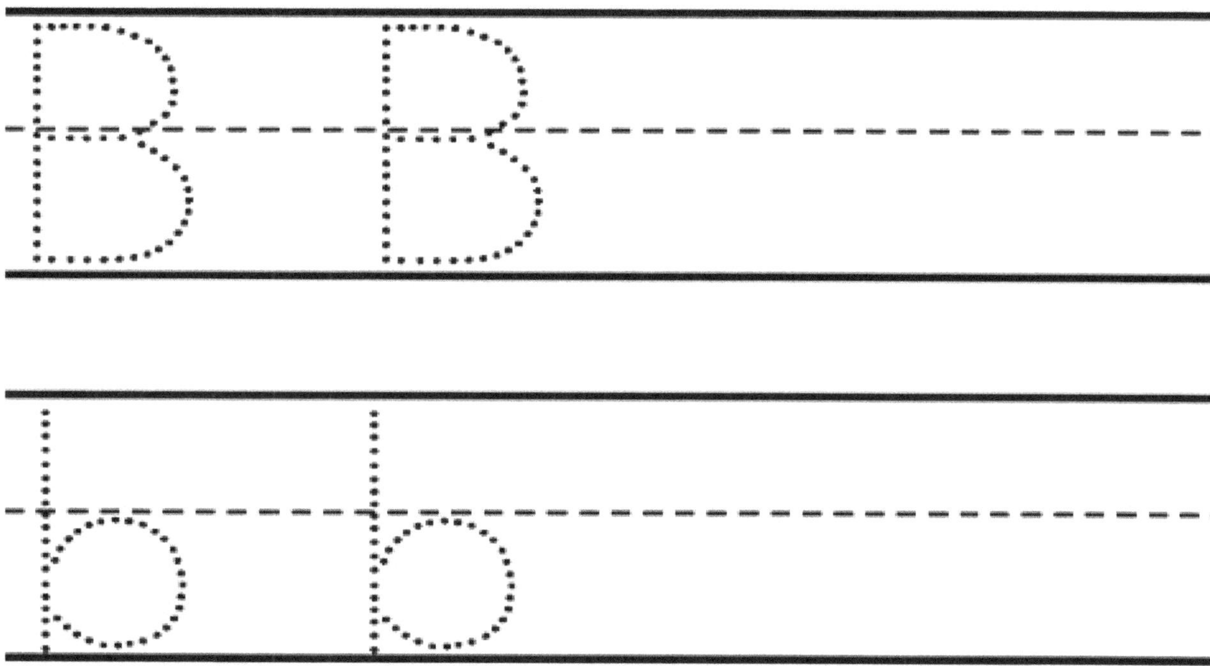

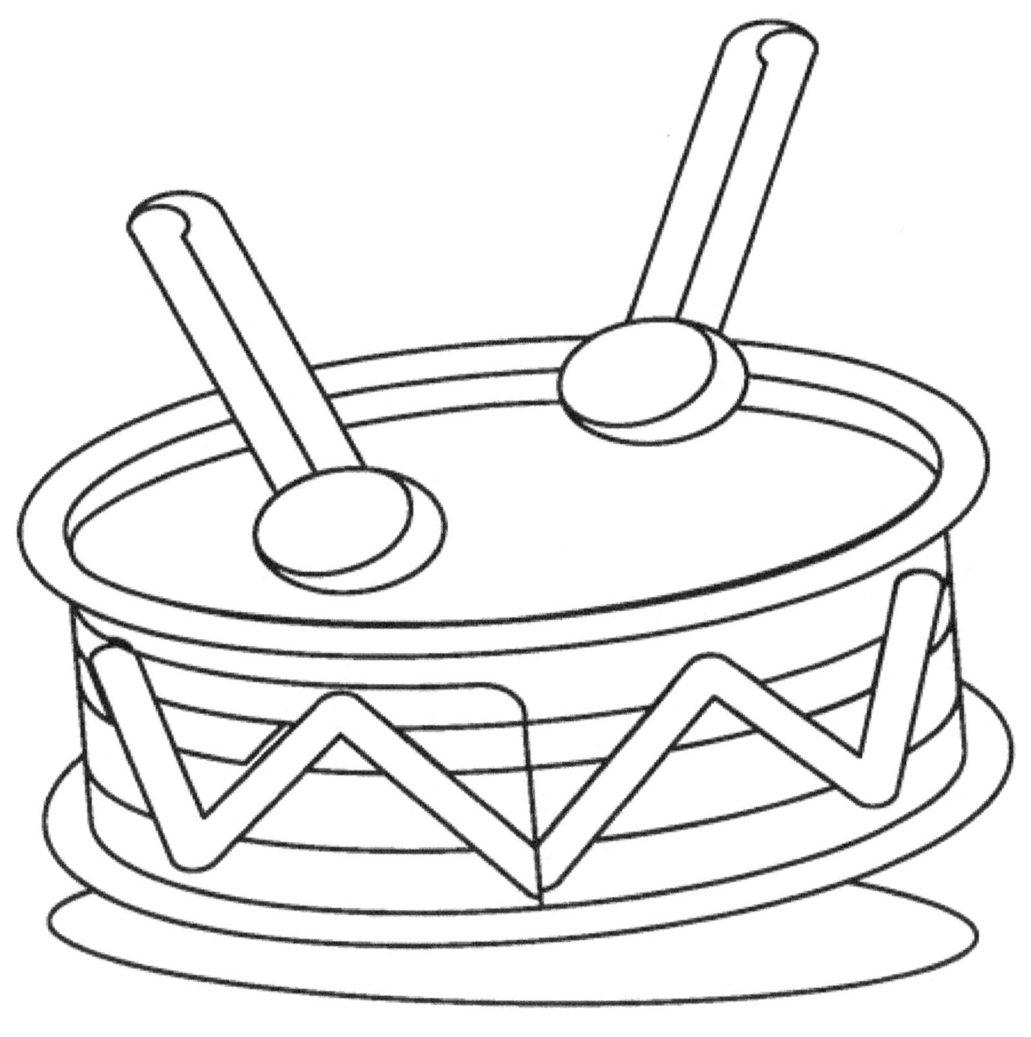

Drum

Elephant

Giraffe
G

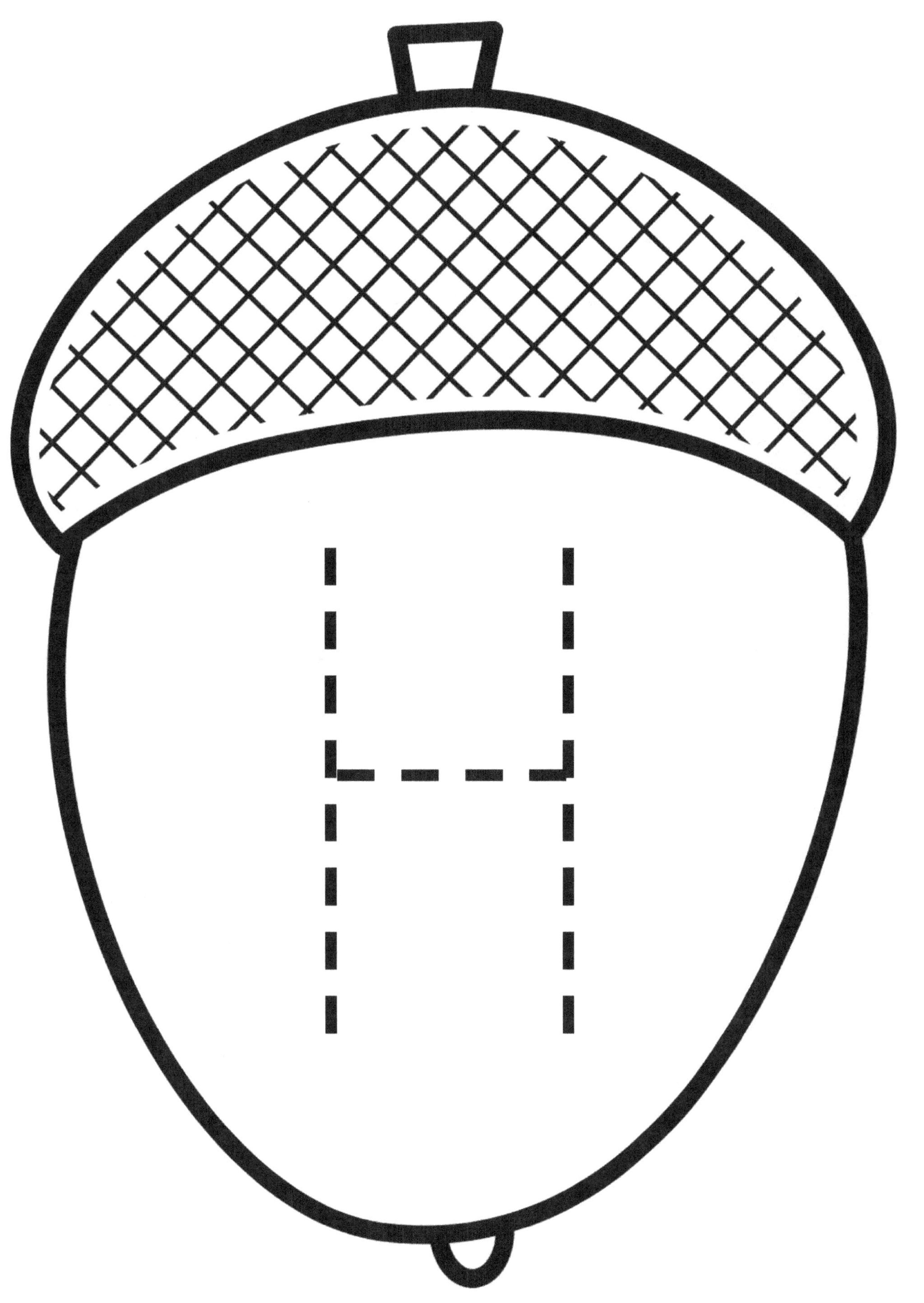

Color the pictures that begin with Ii

K

Lion

M
Mouse
Motorcycle
Monkey

Narwhal

Oo is for onion

Color the pictures that begin with Qq

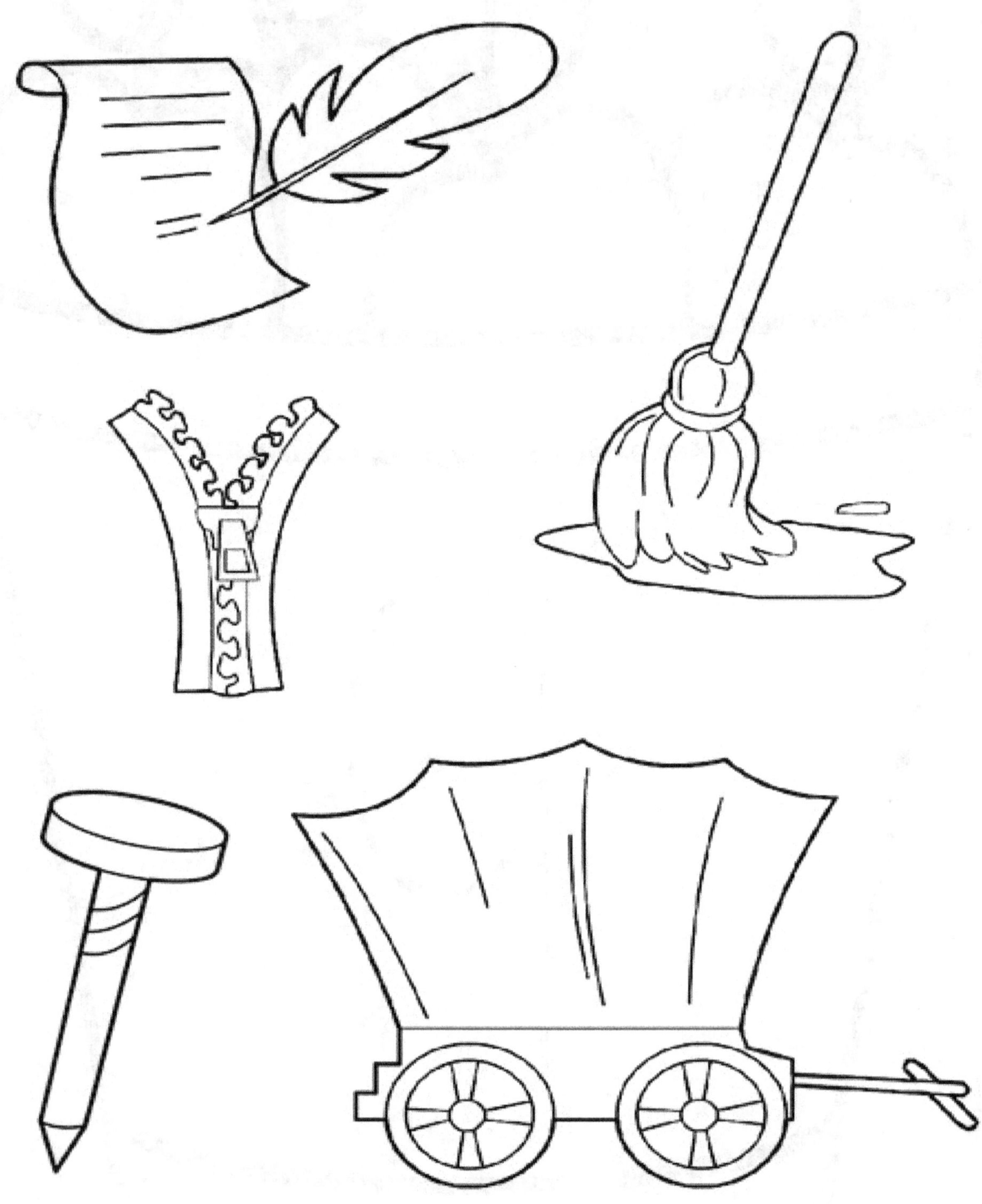

Rr

raccoon

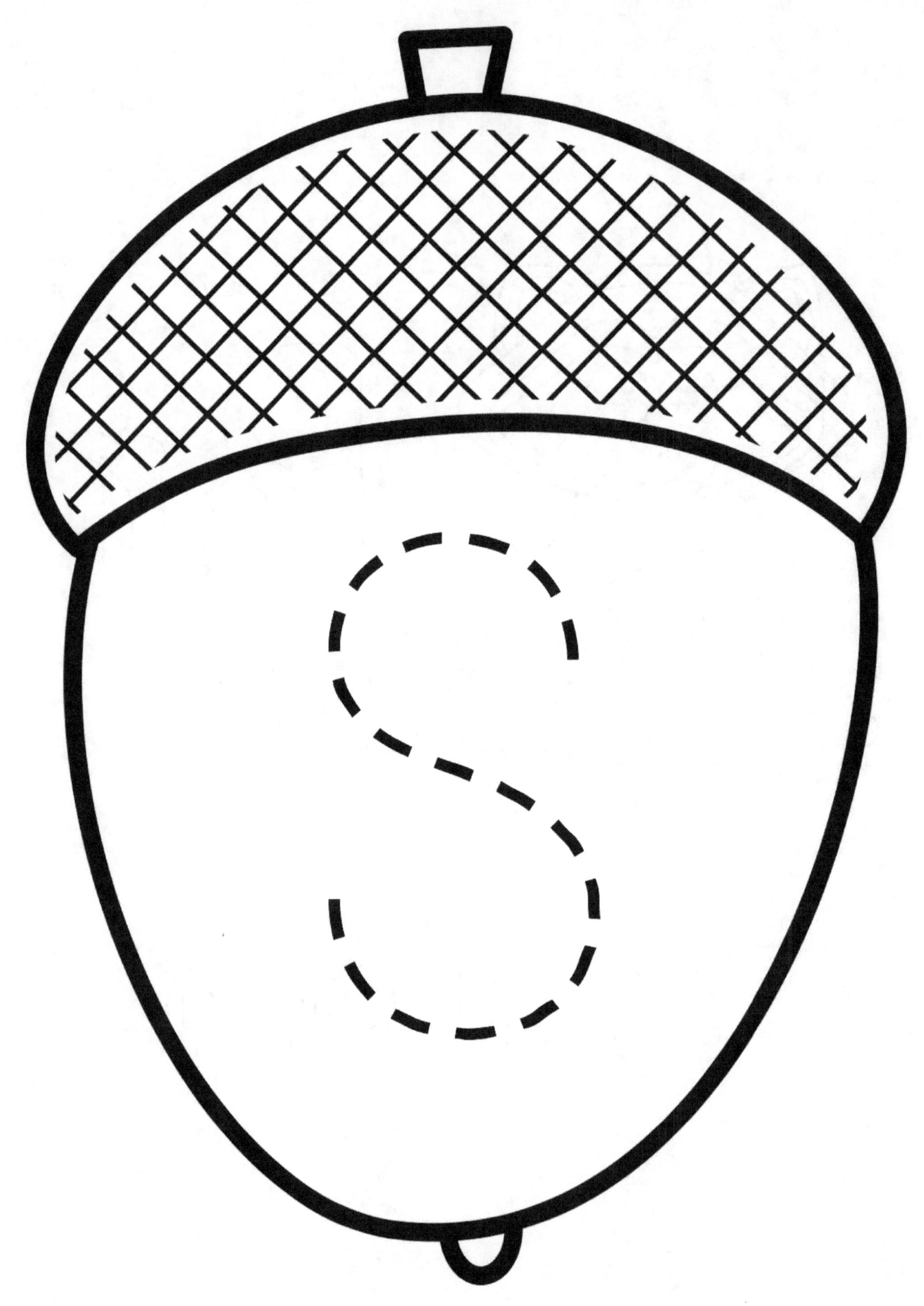

Color the letters Xx

Trace and write the letters Xx

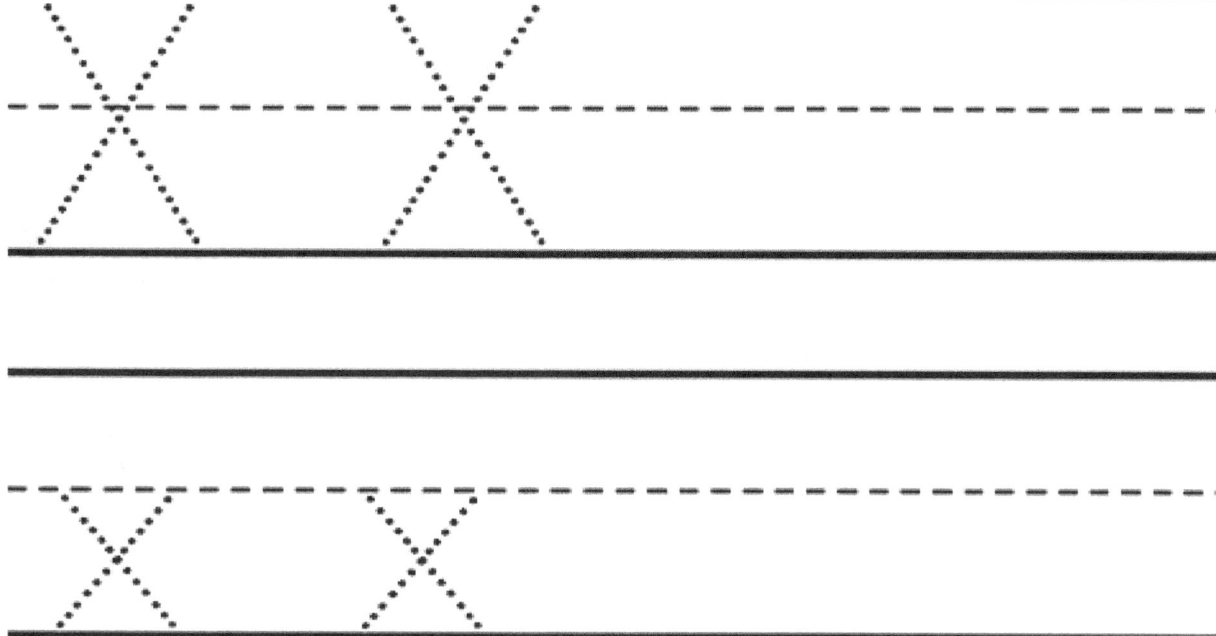

Part n° 02:

26 ALPHABETS

AND

26 ACTIVITIES

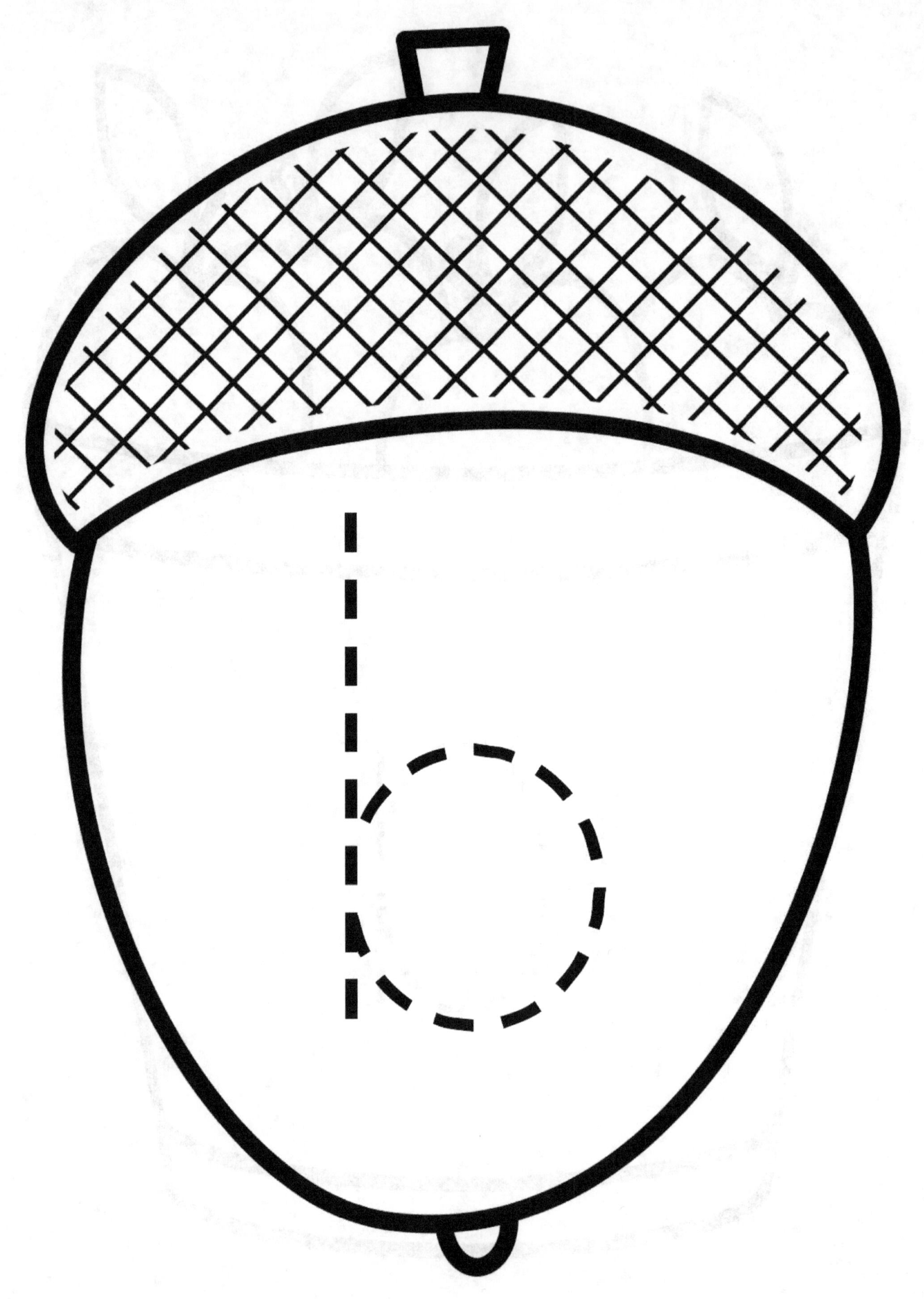

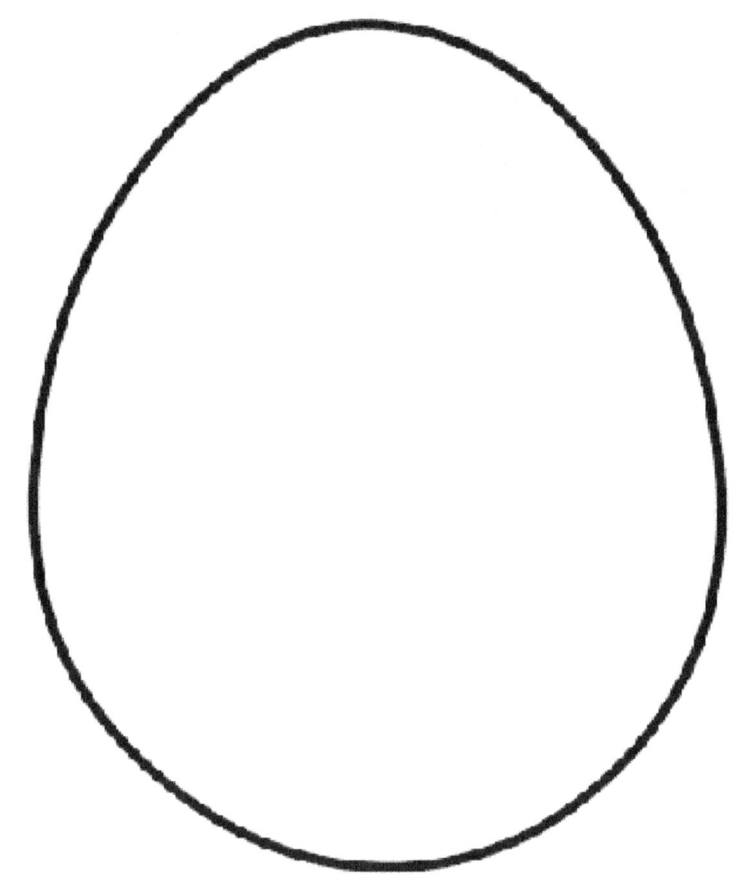

Ee is for egg

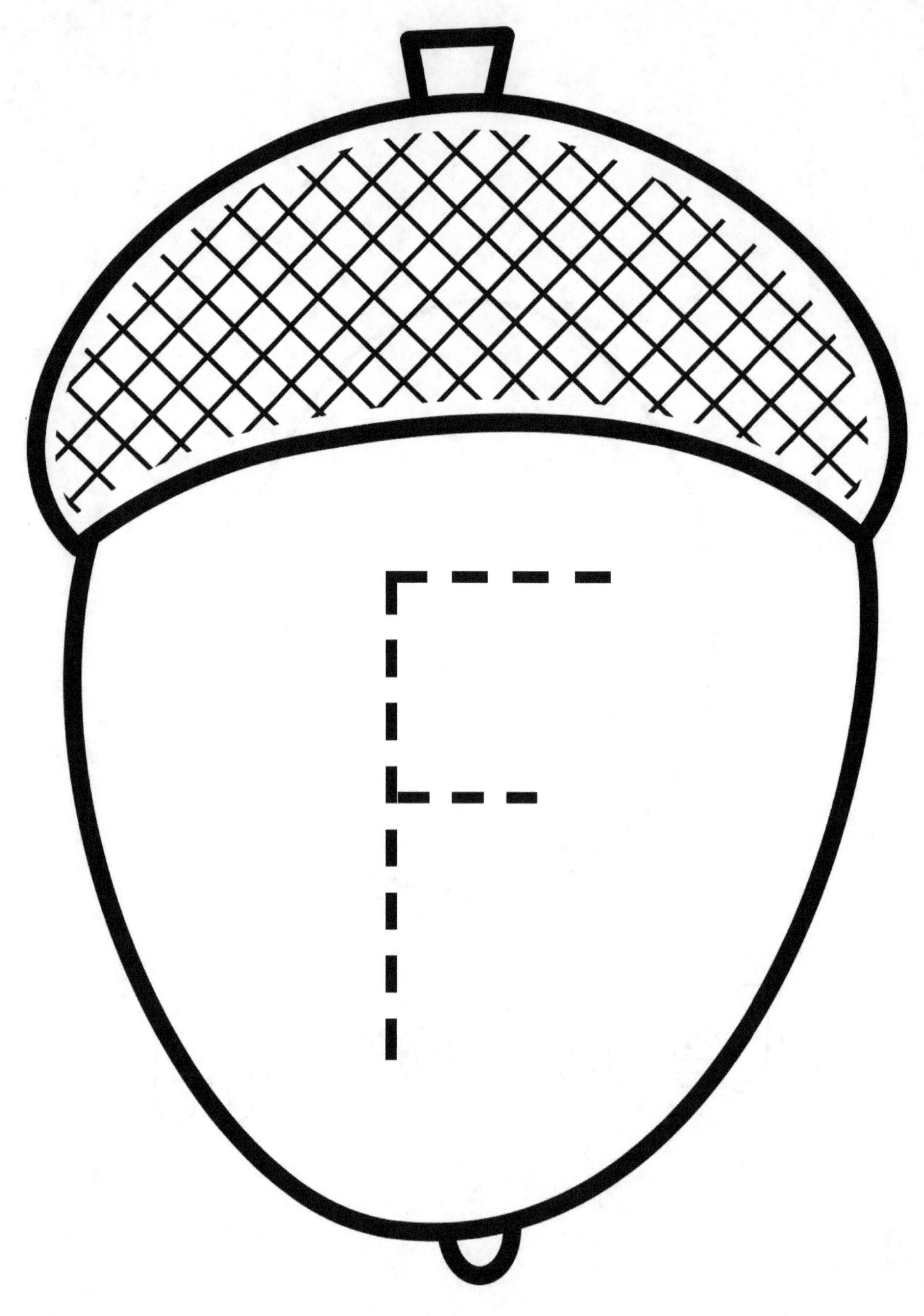

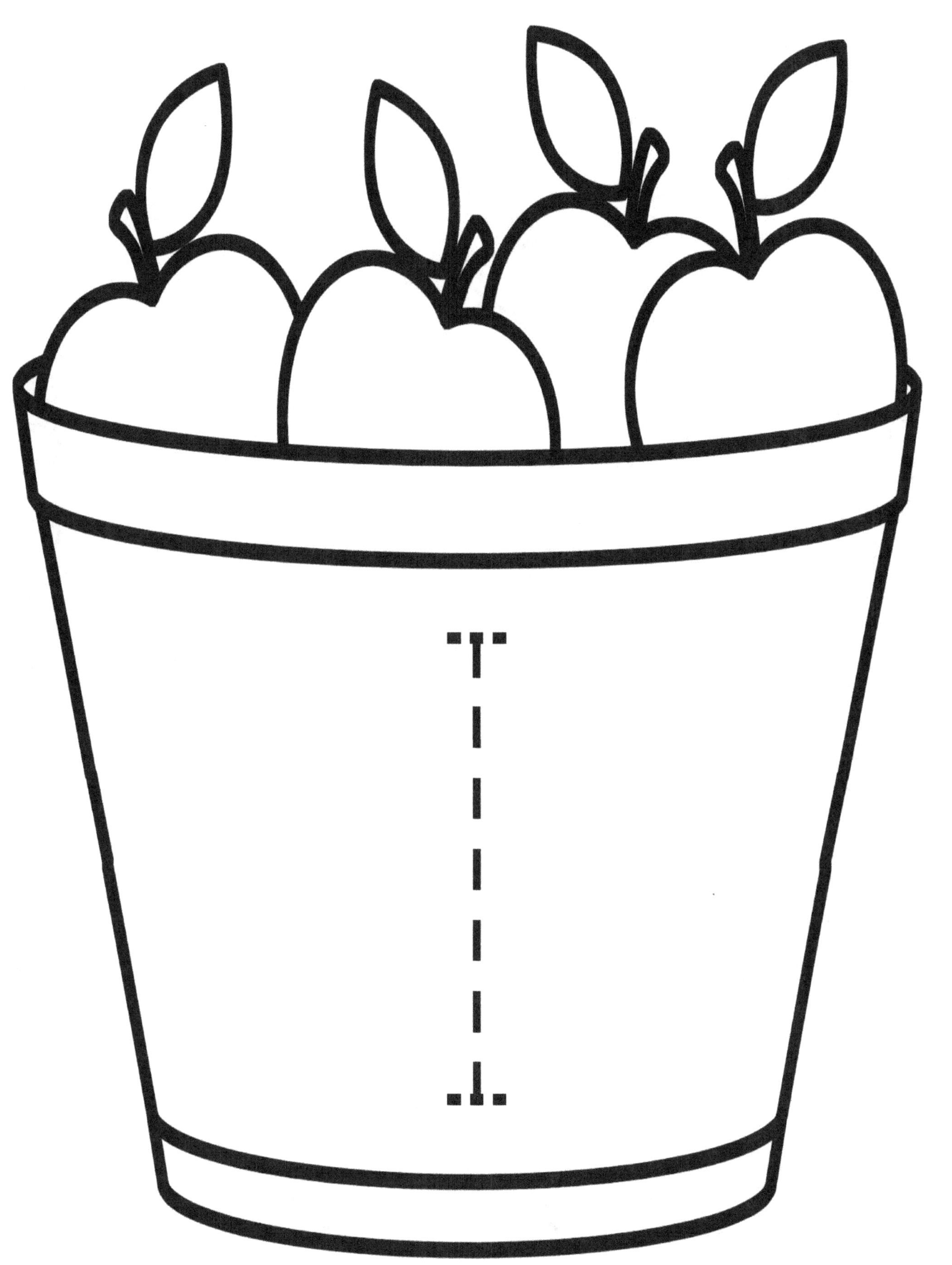

Lion

N

Nest

Color the pictures that begin with Oo

P

Penguin

Qq is For quill

SHEEP

T

TURTLE

Color the letter Uu

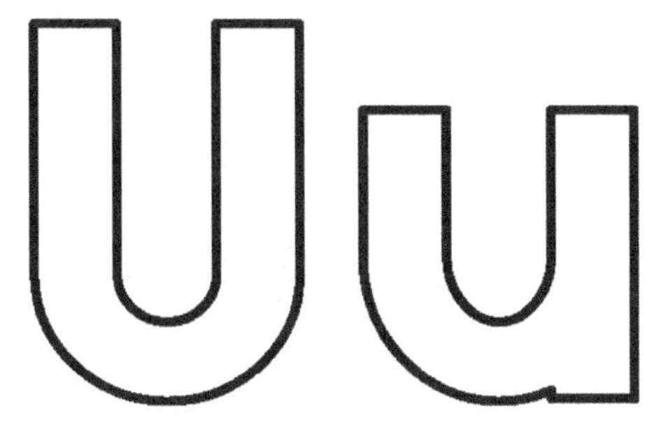

Trace the letter Uu

Color the picture that begins with Uu

Find and color the letter Uu

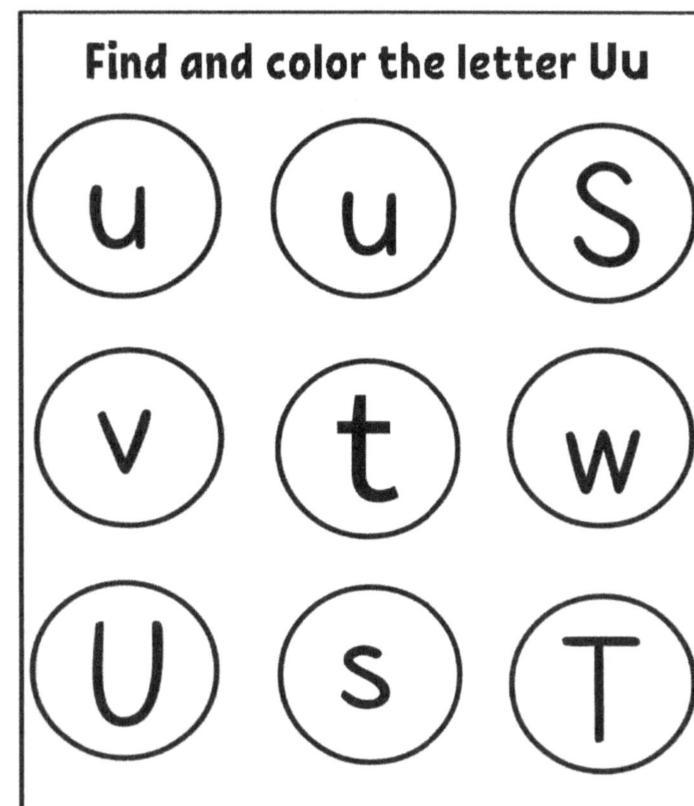

Write the missing letters

S T ☐
s t ☐

Connect it

u •   • u
U •   • U

Ww is for wagon

Yak